Ananda

Inner Bliss

Juhee M

BookLeaf Publishing
India | USA | UK

Made with ❤ on the BookLeaf Publishing Platform
www.bookleafpub.in
www.bookleafpub.com

Dedication

A heart dripping in devotion.

Two big eyes piercing through my soul, searching for my deepest fear. It started flowing out as tears. These precious tears were of an emotion called devotion.
Once it entered my heart, it wanted to grow so the heart kept expanding and circled the universe. Realising this, the heart was so overwhelmed and wrote down poetry to spread these vibrations across to everyone. It had a very unique sweetest fragrance that touched many hearts.
Their hearts also started expanding.

This poetry became an amalgamation of all these hearts beating together for one another and spreading love and joy.

Preface

A love story that deepened their spiritual longing because of a distance.

Before that bond could grow deeper a long pause pressed on their nerves. What was earlier an enchanting difference became a reason to create boundaries. The distance of two countries, of separate cultures and of language drew lines like on sand as two separate teams.

It was not long enough, she started writing poetry to soothe her senses and bridge this void.
The physical distance of two countries could not really fade the longing in their hearts. The un-lived stories swelled up their hearts. They both dealt with an overwhelming situation in their own ways. At first she wrote for herself. And writes every day. Then she writes to become still so that everything fades when she must write. This stillness allows her to hear her heart's sounds. The sounds that are played in his heart's longing.

Those reverberations are frequencies weaving a poetic story between them. Every melody in her heart reminds her of his presence beyond his body. Slowly this presence is very intense, as powerful as getting engulfed into it to be ecstatic. There are signals and forces which mesmerise her at first. Then she knows that he remembered her by a certain sound. She would be pleased to offer a flower or light an oil lamp in the same space everyday and observe the flame. The intensity of that flame assured her of the intensity in love that could not be blown away with winds of peripheral change.

The circumstances do not allow them to meet so this yearning brings out the deeper wisdom and keeps growing and evolves into self annihilation. There is a realisation that this love affair is giving them more than they desired in the beginning.
An enormous amount of trust develops within to keep going and intensifies the spiritual path.

Acknowledgements

Family and friends

Intertwined

It tears me apart to be away from you.

Hearts well connected and
intertwined it felt one.

Who am I to stop them from
beating for one another?

A flowing river in a heart can never dry up.
It would forever flow with love and compassion.

May we both touch the intensity
of every heart beating with passion.

I'm nobody to deny my soul
The love it is longing for...

Hey! Look...
...here it is a piece of my heart
for you and little shining tears of longing
dripping on your eyes from mine.

How can I stop loving you
that's not something in my control.

It's not on the surface so how could
that yearning of heart be fathomed.

There is no use creating boundaries
for depths like these.

Postcards

There was a time of reverence.
There was a time of innocence
There was a time of glances
...through half open windows

There was
...yes there was a time
A time of shyness and newness

Not knowing what would be a lover's
...next steps

There was a time a time of sweetest longings
There was a time

...of out of country
Postcards

Written with Love

Sacred

I'm falling
Falling for you

In this falling
I'm waiting
For you

In this waiting
I'm learning
From you

In this learning
I'm running

Running towards you
To reach out
And touch
Your heart

That heart of gold
And precious stones
The heart of deep gratitude

From valleys of abyssal floor

Of deep oceans

Untouched and
Sacred

Coincidence

Many many rainfalls
...many a droplets

The puddles become wombs
...of falling leaves

Seasons change and
...so does this encounter

Into the realms of soft light
...into depths of oceans

How could it just be a coincidence
...of the one in several hundreds

Muse

Making the most of
...all that's available to me

In an instant and
...sometimes more than that

The swift longing to
...your heart raises my hope

Specially on a night of
...full moon I keep wondering

If I'm in a dream
...of beauty and light

Star

If you look at yourself from my eyes
It's expansive
Limitless
Infinite

Stars do not know
that they are constellations

Speed

Making way for the unknown to enter
Ripping the conditioned shine
Absorbing it all that's gullible

Slowing down

Slowing down

Presence

Be sensitive to the
desires of their heart.

Listen carefully to the sound
of grief in their melancholic voice.

Be there and be present to the worry
they are carrying along while helping you.

Send a message of love
being by their side silently.

...or express and say how you
appreciate their presence in your life.

Namesake

There seems a bridge of vast
...vacant space

That I want to escape at first
...there emerge a sprouting plant

From cracks of your love
...I pluck and let go

Letting go of this grief
...collected over years

Not yours not mine
...ancestral

Naive ness pays off
...with gratitude

And I still look for namesake
...in essence

Heart

Taking deep breaths
...I submerge myself in ART

Making a softer heart
...I take the pilgrim into unknown inner world

Asking you to be part of this journey
...I'm yet to embark fully

Here is a piece of my heart
...that reads

Break it one more time so that
...you can feel, it is in your hands

To protect and shield it
...from your shadow

Listening

Making my heart grow out loud
...enough to make you listen

To my newly written poems
...onto my favourite

Little souvenirs
...lying around like joyous takeaways

Inside the hollow-ness
...of my dancing mud vessel

Called body
...with curves in my case

Come forward to pick up all
...that's yours as a chit in a glass jar

Read it out loud for my
...heart to expand

Making my heart grow out loud
...enough to make you listen

Making my heart grow out loud
...enough to make you listen

Five senses

It is for the senses
... I was pulled into this love affair

I stayed for the roots growing into
...the land beyond sensory perception

Tranquil

My deeper shallow voids
...are making way into this ocean
The other is engulfed
...into this rogue wave
To find wisdom
...at ocean floor

What more is needed
...when I find this tranquil within.

...of bliss

Magic

If there were any
parameters to reach out to...

your hearts beat
I would have really...

Followed the rules
of those straight forward...

Cues.
But there aren't any...
and you know it.

So let me enter
and shine with...

Universal light
of magnificent...

Magical dream.

Devi

Of hearts and vulnerable spaces.
Of minimum talking and more listening.

Of withering personalities into one another.
Of union.
Wisdom.
and
Awakening.

Of standing together by each other's side
...always.
Of making it a spiritual bond.

Who I'm to let go of this
...when Devi blesses me...
Us.

In total abandonment oh lover
...of your silent yet vocal nuances.

Wear your seat belts and hang in there
...for a little while more.

It is going to change the fate of the dreams.

It is coming your way the life
...you would love to live.

Hold tight as it might be a lot to handle.

Be there as I'm always here...

Flute

I'm gushing in pure devotion
but you tell me...

It's entanglement.
I'm way behind my senses...

To comprehend the common as others...
you tell me I'm a fool.

I'm within and outside...
coloured in his love...

You tell me it's madness
said Radha to her Sakhi.

And Krishna smiled...
playing his flute.

Madness

This feeling of dripping in love...
goes beyond my intellect.

A cacophony of sorts
but still melodious...

A madness.

Until I can figure it out...
let me indulge in...

creating art...

For you
Oh divine presence.

Friends

I could cross many rivers...
of boundaries for you.

I could embrace your
imperfections by knitting them...
in my own.

I could jump into fathomless...
lies and truths of friendships.

And could nearly knock over...

a dreamy morning
to see...

That I'm back in time to...
feel this is real.

And now.

Lover

Be a lover...
a lover of all things.

Start with romanticising everything...
and be a lover.

A lover of all...
a lover of everything.

It's a good space to be in.
It's soft and beautiful.

To be in love with everything...
and anything...
around you.

You don't have to make any...
sense out of it just be in love darling.

Dance

We are both Radha
We are both Krishna
We are a woman
We are a man
We are Varaha
A manifestation of divine
You me in eternal union
Of cosmic dance
Darkness intertwined
Into one

Intertwined in one
Still separate entities
Snakes always go level headed

Shaking the limitations
I go into trance
Of making this a magnificent
Ordeals of sorts
But it is still a dance
Of divine embrace

buddy

Making you my giggle buddy
And splash splash the puddles we
Jump into
Everyday to see the charm
In this beautiful sparkling
Life
Come along